OXFORD
UNIVERSITY PRESS

Great Clarendon Street, Oxford OX2 6DP

Oxford University Press is a department of the University of Oxford.
It furthers the University's objective of excellence in research, scholarship,
and education by publishing worldwide in

Oxford New York

Athens Auckland Bangkok Bogotá Buenos Aires
Cape Town Chennai Dar es Salaam Delhi Florence Hong Kong Istanbul
Karachi Kolkata Kuala Lumpur Madrid Melbourne Mexico City Mumbai
Nairobi Paris São Paulo Shanghai Singapore Taipei Tokyo Toronto Warsaw

with associated companies in Berlin Ibadan

Oxford is a registered trade mark of Oxford University Press
in the UK and in certain other countries

Database right Oxford University Press (maker)

First published 2001

British Library Cataloguing in Publication Data available

ISBN 0-19-276264-8 (hardback)
ISBN 0-19-276265-6 (paperback)

1 3 5 7 9 10 8 6 4 2

Typeset by Mary Tudge

Printed in Hong Kong

Cockadoodle Moo

Compiled by **John Foster**

OXFORD

Contents

Late One Night In Kalamazoo

Late one night in Kalamazoo,
the baboons had a barbecue,
the kudus flew a green balloon,
the poodles yodelled to the moon.

A monkey strummed a blue guitar;
a donkey caught a falling star,
a camel danced with a kangaroo,
late one night in Kalamazoo.

Jack Prelutsky

11

Adelaide Ida

Adelaide Ida the dancing spider
Dances in the morning
With the sun beside her,
Dances in the evening
As the shadows hide her
Dancing, d
      a
       n
        g
         l
          i
           n
            g
             Adelaide Ida.

Daphne Kitching

Tarantula

She's hairy.
She's scary,
She's covered in bristles.
A fighter,
A biter,
With legs like eight thistles.

A muncher,
A cruncher,
With greedy jaws gnashing.
A mawler,
A crawler . . .

But I think she's SMASHING!

Clare Bevan

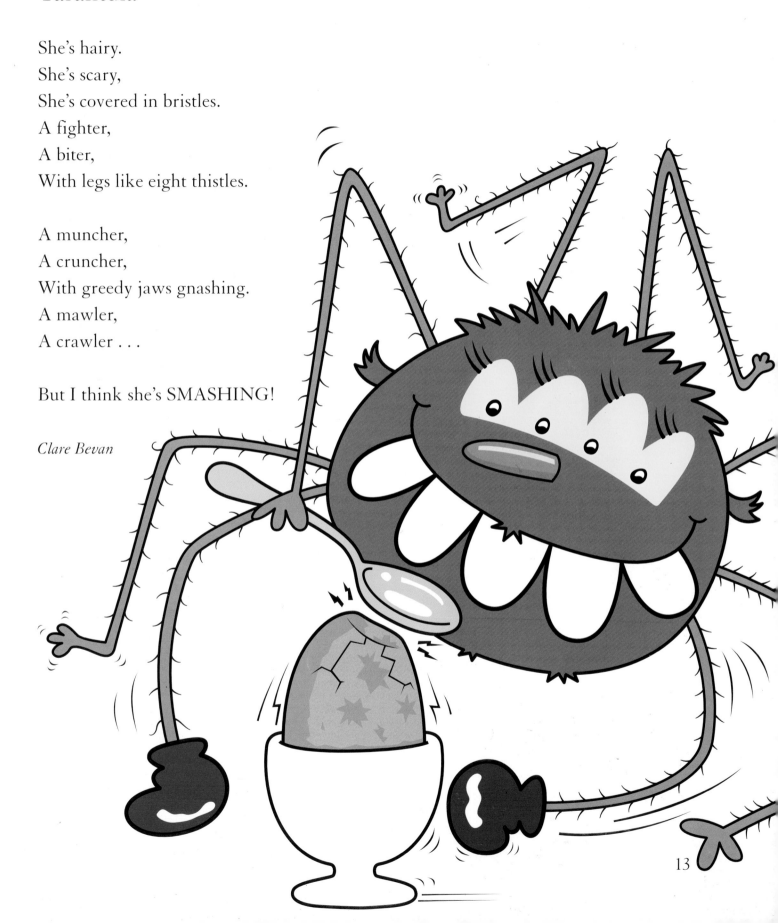

13

Jessica June

Jessica June
And her birthday balloon
Went flying right up
To the silvery moon.

The Man in the Moon
Blinked his eyes in surprise,
When Jessica June
Floated up through the skies.

'Let's have a party,'
he said, with a smile.
'No one has been here
for such a long while.'

So he made her a moon-cake
All sprinkled with stars.
Then they sat on a moonbeam
And flew off to Mars.

The little space children
All wanted to play
At passing the parcel
And spinning the tray.

But soon it was bed-time
And Jessica June
Had to whizz back to Earth
With her birthday balloon.

As she climbed into bed,
She smiled up at the moon,
And sleepily whispered,
'I'm coming back soon.'

14

Cynthia Rider

Mr Hullabaloo

Mr Hullabaloo went to bed in a shoe
and he travelled around by balloon.
He wore a tall hat
and he kept a pink cat
and played snap with the man in the moon.

Marian Swinger

15

If I Were an Explorer

If I were an explorer
I'd reach that far-off land
Called Jumbledup, where sand was sea
And sea was made of sand,
Where snow fell every summer
On herds of grazing bees
And cows flew round the blossom
Of the orange apple trees.

Richard Edwards

Dangerous

When we're
Hunting
We explore
Squares upon the
kitchen floor;
We must
Get from
Here to there
Without touching
Anywhere;
For this
Square is
Safe for us.
But that one is
Dangerous.

Dorothy Aldis

17

The Magic Carpet

Come and ride on me,
I can take you where
Wizards weave spells
In the evening air.

Come and ride on me,
I can show you caves
Of shining treasure
Beneath the cold waves.

Come and ride on me,
I can show you places
Where dinosaurs dance
And dragons run races.

Come and ride on me
Through skies that gleam
With a thousand and one
Enchanted dreams.

Cynthia Rider

Fancy Dress Parade

Kenny is a pirate
With a skull and crossbones hat
Tammy's sweating buckets—
She's a furry ginger cat.
Dan's a scary Dracula
Sam is Super Ted
Lisa's got the giggles
As a loaf of crusty bread.
Anne's a fairy princess
Ben's a crafty spy
I'm red and black and spotty
Tell me, what am I?

Patricia Leighton

The Ballpool

In the ballpool you can float
In coloured balls, just like a moat
Around the climbing frame and slide,
Over plastic waves you glide.

When you've swum the lumpy sea
And climbed back out in time for tea,
Look back, see how the ocean calms
Without your thrashing legs and arms!

Coral Rumble

Oh, Take Me To the Seaside!

Oh, take me to the seaside
On a day just like today
To smell the tang of seaweed,
Feel the stinging of the spray,
To see the breakers, taste the salt
And hear the crash of foam—
Please take me to the seaside
Then forget to take me home!

Sue Cowling

Sand Castle

I built a house
   One afternoon
With bucket, cup,
   And fork and spoon,

Then scooped a shovel-
   ful of shore
On top to add
   The second floor.

But when the fingers
   Of the sea
Reached up and waved
   A wave to me,

It tumbled down
   Like dominoes
And disappeared
   Between my toes.

J. Patrick Lewis

23

Sounds Like Magic

I listened to a seashell
and thought I could hear
the rushing of the waves
inside my ear.

I held an empty eggshell
close against my head
and thought I heard a pecking chick
hatching from its bed.

I found a hollow coconut
and listened for a sound
and thought I heard horses' hooves
pounding on the ground.

I took an empty teacup
to see what I might hear
and thought I heard a giant's voice
booming in my ear.

Celia Warren

24

The Scary Fairies

There's a cave in the wood
Where the scary fairies hide,
And one day, when I'm bigger,
I'm going to peep inside.

And when those scary fairies
With their silver-shining eyes
See me standing looking at them
They will have a big surprise.

They will think I'm very fierce
And they'll squeal and run away.
But that's for when I'm very big . . .
I'm much too small today!

Cynthia Rider

25

Pumpkin Pumpkin

Pumpkin
Pumpkin
Where have you been?

I been to Hallowe'en
to frighten the queen

Pumpkin
Pumpkin
how did you do it?

With two holes for my eyes
and a light
in me head

I frightened the queen
right under her bed!

John Agard

Green-eyed Witches

Down in the woods where the trees are bare
And twigs scritch scratch to tangle your hair,
There in the light of a sliver of moon
The green-eyed witches sit and croon
In tattered capes and pointed hats
Around a cauldron filled with bats,
They fly on broomsticks way up high
To sweep dark cobwebs from the sky.
And catch giant spiders for a brew . . .
At Hallowe'en—they might snatch you!

Georgie Adams

Winter Weather

I like it when the night is dark
when street lights start to glow,
like strings of pretty amber beads
where shadows stretch and grow.

I like it when the rain is black
when it makes a pattering sound,
like a thousand needles falling fast
into puddles on the ground.

I like it in the middle of town,
when winter coats our street,
when snow falls soft as feathers
and you can't hear people's feet.

I like it when the wind is wild
and I love the song of the storm,
dry leaves dancing across the park
when I'm safe inside—and warm!

Moira Andrew

Snow In the Lamplight

From my bedroom,
In bare feet,
I look through curtains,
Down the street
To the lamp-post
There below,
Lighting up
The falling snow.
Snow like feathers
In the light,
Like some gigantic
Pillow-fight.
Will it settle?
I'm hoping so.
Drifting,
Sledging,
Snowball snow.

Mark Burgess

Footprints

We went out, and in the night
All the world had turned to white.
Snowy garden, snowy hedge,
Ice along the window ledge.
And all around the garden seat
A tiny bird with tiny feet
Had left his footprints in the snow,
As he went hopping to and fro.

Shirley Hughes

Snowman Snow

Come and wade
In soft wet snow.
Roll and shape it:
Snowman snow.

Big round belly—
Make it grow.
Roll and pack it:
Snowman snow.

Now the head,
And place it so.
Pat and pack it:
Snowman snow.

Edith E. Cutting

Fun In the Snow

Hop-a-long,
Skip-a-long,
Slip-a-long,
Run.

We're out in the snow,
Let's have some fun.

Up-a-long,
Down-a-long,
Skid-a-long,
Whoops!

We're sliding along
And down we swoop.

Rush-a-long,
Swish-a-long,
Swoosh-a-long,
Slide.

We're on our sledges
And down we ride.

Cynthia Rider

31

At Christmas

Quickly—hide it! Hide it!
Softly you must go,
silently and secretly
creeping to and fro . . .
nobody must see you,
nobody must hear . . .
Quickly! Quick—they're coming—
someone's drawing near!

Stop the paper crackling—
wait, and hold your hand.
Hide away the parcel—
don't they understand
it is nearly Christmas?
Help me tie the string.
Nobody must guess we're
up to ANYthing . . .

Jean Kenward

Christmas

Carol-singing in the frosty air,
Holly wreaths all down the stair.
Reindeer galloping across the night,
Ivy looped with tinsel bright.
Stockings hung on ends of beds,
Trees decorated in golds and reds.
Mince pies ready, spicy and hot,
A baby in a manger cot.
Stars to guide kings all the way . . .
. . . And we wake up to Christmas Day!

Moira Andrew

Jiggery Street

On Jiggery Street
the children fly;
the sun drops candy
from the sky.

The pillar box
has learned to walk;
eats the letters
with a knife and fork.

Doorbells whistle,
windows wink,
dishes jump
from the sink,

dustbins whirl
like spinning tops;
babies cheer,
the hedges hop!

So wear three hats
upon your head;
paint your
Sunday buttons red;

put sparky slippers
on your feet,
come for a walk
down Jiggery Street.

Irene Rawnsley

Jiggery Jaggery

Jiggery, Jaggery
gingerbread

tap your feet,
nod your head.

Makes you dance,
makes you fly—

gingerbread bopping
round the sky.

Joan Poulson

35

Gloves

My gloves are in a muddle
And I'm trying to sort them out.
I turned them to the other side
But now they're inside out!

I tried to turn them back again
But now it seems to me
That where there were five fingers
There now are only three!

Brenda Williams

Night Lights

My aunt gave me luminous laces
Exactly the kind I'd choose
They're a wonderful kind of invention
For cheering up tired old shoes
I don't wear them on any old outing
To school or play in the park
I wear them at night when I'm frightened
Cos they switch themselves on in the dark.

Hiawyn Oram

37

Liquorice Bootlaces

I tie my boots with liquorice.
It is a pleasant thing
To eat the pieces when they snap.
They're tastier than string.

Irene Rawnsley

Tiny Diny

Dear, oh dear,
oh, what shall I do?
There's a tiny little dinosaur
in my shoe.

Her teeth are sharp
and her head's like a rock
When I put my foot in,
she chewed my sock.

Her skin is rough
and her tail is long.
And her ripply muscles
are ever so strong.

And I want to go out,
but what can I do
with a tiny little dinosaur
in my shoe?

Tony Mitton

Holiday Memories

When I was on holiday
I went to Timbuktu,
I wrestled with a jaguar
And boxed a kangaroo.

I journeyed into jungles,
I swam the deepest sea,
I climbed the highest mountain
And a monkey-puzzle tree,

I chatted to a seagull,
I met a big baboon,
I floated on a moonbeam
Until I reached the moon.

I visited the planets,
I lit up all the stars,
I gossiped to a parrot
Travelling to Mars.

I sailed across the ocean,
I drove a Greyhound bus,
I rode across the desert
On a hippopotamus.

I heard a mermaid singing,
I fought a killer shark,
I grappled with a Grizzly
In a wild Safari Park.

I chased a band of pirates
Completely round the bend.
And now the summer's over
And so is this—THE END.

June Crebbin

Riddle

I can whistle
a tune.
I can sing.
I can croon.

I'm a friend
to the trees.
I'm a buzz
for the bees.

On a night
dark and deep
I will keep
you from sleep

When I mutter
and roar
and moan
round your door.

I'm as wild
as a lion
or mild
as a lamb . . .

Do you know
who I am?

Ann Bonner

42

On Windy Days

On windy days we take our kites,
Unwind the strong, thin strings,
And soon the sky is full of shapes
Of floating, coloured wings.

As paper birds and butterflies,
Orange and gold and red,
Fly in the air until the wind
Decides to go to bed.

Daphne Lister

43

The Cloud Dragon

Looking up at the sky
I see a cloud dragon passing by
Changing shapes as he goes
Breathing fire from his nose

He opens his jaws and just for fun
Moves to swallow up the sun
The sky grows dark—it will rain, no doubt
Please, dragon, spit the sun back out.

John Coldwell

44

Rain

Can you see the grey cloud
Up in the sky?
His face is so sad
He is starting to cry.

Roger Stevens

Mister Frog

Mister Frog
Jumped out of the pond
Into the pouring rain.
He said, 'My word, it's cold and wet,'
So he jumped back in again.

Arthur Smith

Mud

There's a muddy little puddle
By the duckpond on our farm,
With squeedgy, squidgy mud in it
That trickles down my arm.
It squelches through my fingers,
And in between my toes;
I can't think how it happens
But mud gets up my nose.
My hair has sludgy lumps of it
It splatters round my eyes . . .
There's always loads of mud on ME
When I make my mud pies.

Georgie Adams

Rainy Day Rumpus!

Boys and girls come out to play,
Pull on your wellies without delay!
Jump in a puddle and splash your gran
Then scamper away as fast as you can!

Judith Nicholls

I Met a Lion In the Park

I met a lion in the park,
I took him home for tea,
But when I fed him bread and jam
He wouldn't play with me.

I met a camel in the rain,
We both got very wet,
But when I took him home to Mum,
He wouldn't be my pet.

I met a monkey in the street,
She had a baby, too,
But when I asked them home to lunch,
They went to Timbuktu.

I met my daddy at the shop,
He'd bought me a surprise.
It had a little curly tail,
And big brown puppy eyes.

Lucy Coats

At the Playground

When we went to the playground
I swung on the swings,
I slid on the slide,
I hung from the rings.
I raced over to Mum
for a kiss and a cuddle,
but as we were leaving,
I fell in a puddle!

Brian Moses

If I Were a Dog

If I were a dog
I'd stare and pout
until you felt guilty
and took me out.

I'd leap and lunge
and roll and race,
then walk you home
and lick your face.

Bob Morrow

Marvel Paws

Marvel Paws
is a magic cat.
She dreams up spells
on the kitchen mat.
She walks the length
of the garden wall.
Then POP!
she isn't there
at all . . .

Marvel Paws
is a flicker of fur,
a rustle of grass
and a quiet purr.
Marvel Paws
is an empty dish,
an upset jug
and a missing fish.

Marvel Paws
is a magic cat.
She has no cloak
or magic hat.
But I know by the way
her whiskers twitch
that Marvel Paws
is a pussycat witch.

Tony Mitton

Hide and Seek

...Eight...Nine...Ten!
That's the lot.
Here I come,
ready or not!

I'm the cat,
you're the mouse.
I stalk slowly
through the house,
seeking under,
in, behind.
Great big mouse,
you're hard to find!

Getting warmer.
You're in there!
I heard a squeak
behind the chair!
Now you're trapped,
you can't run.
Watch me pounce.
Here I come!

Count to ten,
don't try to peek.
My turn to hide.
Your turn to seek.

Jane Clarke

52

Blowing Bubbles

Dip your pipe and gently blow.
Watch the tiny bubble grow
Big and bigger, round and fat,
Rainbow-coloured, and then—
SPLAT!

Margaret Hillert

53

Clap Your Hands

Clap your hands
Above your head—
Wake up, wake up,
Sleepyhead.

Clap your hands
Behind your back.
Make a click
And then a clack.

Clap your hands
From side to side.
Hold your arms out
Very wide.

Clap hands fast
With your best friend.
Now our game
Is at an end!

Pam Gidney

54

Swinging

Daddy swings me round and round
like a searchlight beam.
Will he stop
or will he drop me
as I laugh and scream?

Round and round
above the ground;
the wind runs through my hair,
trees and grass
rush up and pass.
I'm as light as air.

Now much slower—round, round.
Now I'm going lower, lower—
till I touch the ground.

Jill Townsend

Only Human

Ben said he was a chimpanzee
Swinging through the trees
But then because he's human
He fell and grazed his knees.

Hiawyn Oram

Woodpecker

Woodpecker, woodpecker
Tapping at the tree
Woodpecker, woodpecker
Can't you see?
Woodpecker, woodpecker
You can't win
You can knock all day
But there's no one in!

Brenda Williams

56

The Nest

Don't move
  don't touch
don't speak
  do you see
a blackbird's nest
  in the holly tree?

Look very carefully
  in between
last year's prickle
  and this year's green . . .

Timid and brown
  the mother bird
listens and watches.
  Has she heard?

Whisper—
  whisper—
do you see
a blackbird's nest
  in the holly tree?

Jean Kenward

Grasshopper One

Grasshopper one
Grasshopper two
Grasshopper hopping
in the morning dew

Grasshopper three
Grasshopper four
Grasshopper stopping
by the leafy door

Grasshopper five
Grasshopper six
Grasshopper lying
like a green matchstick

Grasshopper seven
Grasshopper eight
Grasshopper suddenly
standing up straight

Grasshopper nine
Grasshopper ten
Grasshopper,
   will you be my
      secret friend?

Grace Nichols

The Underworld

When I am lying in the grass
I watch the ants and beetles pass;
And once I lay so very still
A mole beside me built a hill.

Margaret Lavington

I Wish I Was a Centipede

I wish I was a centipede.
I'd *wriggle* under roots,
And spend each evening polishing
My hundred muddy boots.
I'd build myself a little home
Beneath the mossy rocks
And spend each morning washing out
My hundred smelly socks.

Kaye Umansky

Pleas-e!

Bumble bee, bumble bee,
Fly away home;
Leave my naked toes
Alone!

Bumble bee, bumble bee,
Don't you know
Another place where
You can go?

Bumble bee, bumble bee,
When I doze off,
I don't need you, so
Buzz off!

June Crebbin

High on the Wall

High on the wall
Where the pennywort grows
Polly Penwarden
Is painting her toes.

One is purple
And two are red
And two are the colour
Of her golden head.

One is blue
And two are green
And the others are the colours
They've always been.

Charles Causley

Grandad's Greenhouse

When I stay with Grandad
He says 'Now come with me,'
And takes me to the greenhouse
Down the garden, past the tree.
It's the magic world of Grandad,
Full of pots, and plants all growing,
Watering cans and spades and hoes,
Soil, and seeds for sowing,

In Grandad's greenhouse.

Between the plants he has a chair
Where he can sit and think,
Or read his newspaper or sing,
Or rest to have his drink.
A different world of quietness,
It looks and smells, well—*green*,
We plant and weed till Grandma calls,
And *she* knows where we've been . . .

In Grandad's greenhouse.

Daphne Kitching

Grandma's House

Grandma's house is very small
just a bedroom and a hall

and a parlour full of flowers
lots of clocks to tell the hours

and a kitchen with a cat
fast asleep upon a mat

and a bathroom cool and white
full of towels soft and bright

and a front door with a bell
and a garden with a well

and a place to sit and dream
down beside a little stream.

Grandma's house is full of things
things with wheels and things with wings,

things with spouts and things with handles,
bells and books and fans and candles.

Grandma's house is very small,
but I love to go to call,

and to share a pot of tea—
just my grandmama and me!

Pamela Mordecai

Rock-A-Bye

Rock-a-bye baby
In our front room,
I'm taking care of you
This afternoon.

Mum's in the kitchen
Chatting with Gran,
I shall amuse you
As well as I can.

Do you like water
To splish-splosh your toes?
Do you like paint
On the end of your nose?

Do you like building
Up to the sky
Then knocking the bricks down?
Baby, don't cry.

I know what you'll like—
To bang this big drum.
I thought that would please you . . .
Ooooh, sorry, Mum.

Frances Nagle

Rockabye Baby

Rockabye baby
    On the stairtop,
Crying and screaming
    When will she stop?
Is it her temper?
    The way that she's pinned?
Rockabye baby
    It's simply the wind.

Max Fatchen

What's In the Inbox?

I'm here by the computer
But it isn't my turn yet:
Mum's online and shopping
On the Internet.
I am a bit excited
Cos I can't wait to see
If there's anything
In the Inbox for me.

Mum's finished. Now it's my turn.
Fingers crossed for a surprise!
I sent e-mails this morning
And I'm waiting for replies.
So here I go . . . two mouse clicks . . .
It's like magic . . . and yippee!
There's a message
In the Inbox for me!

Eric Finney

Fi! Fo! Fum! Fee!

Fi! Fo! Fum! Fee!
I sniff a big plate of chips for my tea.
Be they with fishball or burger or egg
I'll pour on the ketchup till everything's red.

Lucy Coats

Miss One, Two, and Three

Miss One, Two, and Three
Could never agree
On what kind of buns
They should have for their tea.
Miss One preferred currants,
Miss Two preferred plain,
Miss Three ate the lot
And was sick on the train.

Kaye Umansky

69

Noisy Food

When you're munching crunchy apples
or you're slurping up your soup,
when you're eating crackly crisps
all on your own or in a group,
when you're crunching up your cornflakes
or you're popping bubblegum,
or you're sucking at an orange
with such squelches that your mum
says, 'Can't you eat more quietly,
that noise is rather rude!'
It's then you say, 'It's not my fault.
I'm eating noisy food.'

Marian Swinger

crackle crackle

slurp slurp

crunch crunch

crisps

70

There Once Was an Old Man From York

There once was an old man from York
Who tried to eat soup with a fork.
'This is taking a while,'
He said with a smile,
'No wonder I'm thin as a stalk.'

Sue Graves

What Would You Do?

What would you do if your sausages flew
And your peas danced around on the plate?

Would you still eat if your carrots had feet
And twirled one leg raised on a skate?

What would you drink if your tea turned pink
And started to sing a loud song?
Would you join in the chorus along with the tea?
Would you have a wild dance with the friendliest pea?

Or skate with a carrot or skip with the fruit,
Or land with a sausage by egg parachute?

I know what I'd do—with the loudest 'Yahoo!'
I'd turn cartwheels and yell out, 'How's that?'
Then I'd run out and play with my dinner all day
And what would I eat? Why, my hat!

Michelle Magorian

72

Clumsy Clementina

Clumsy Clementina
Tripped over the cat.
Up flew her ice-cream,
Oops!
Bump!
Splat!
Cone in her ear,
Ice-cream on her clothes,
And a chocolate flake
Up
Her
Nose!

Kaye Umansky

A Glance at the Menu

Potatoes in their jackets
With the special of the day?
Potatoes in their jackets?
Whatever next? I say.
Sprouts in their pyjamas?
Tomatoes dressed in shirts?
Peas in tartan anoraks?
Broccoli in skirts?
Cauliflower with socks on?
Baseball-capped green beans?
Onions wearing overcoats?
Carrots wearing jeans?

Potatoes in their jackets? No,
I don't want dressed-up food.
Waiter, bring me something else,
And this time something nude.

Richard Edwards

One For the Pineapple

One for the pineapple for our tea.
Two for the plums in the old plum tree.
Three for the empty banana skins.
Four for the peach juice on our chins.
Five for a bunch of bright red cherries.
Six for a handful of ripe blackberries.
Seven for the apples in the pie Dad made.
Eight for the lemons in the lemonade.
Nine for the oranges we squeezed for squash.
Ten for the fingers that need a wash.

John Foster

Plain To See?

My first is in coffee and also in cake.
My second's in honey that busy bees make.
My third is in orange and also in oats.
My fourth is in cabbage but never in goats.
My fifth is in olive but never in greens.
My sixth is in lemon but not found in beans.
My seventh's in almond but not in frogs' legs.
My eighth is in tea but absent from eggs.
My last's in éclair and also in cream.

Is it plain you like eating the food in this scheme?

John Kitching

Like Who . . . ?

Grandpa says I've got Mum's eyes,
Mum says I'm like my dad,
Dad says his ears stick out too much
And mine are just as bad.

But when I look in the mirror
All that I can see
Is someone pretty neat and cool
Who only looks like ME!

Celia Warren

Reflections

In my mirror
I often see
someone who
looks just like me!

He never seems
to brush his hair,
he dresses in
my underwear.

He must be shy
because he hides
whenever I
look round the sides.

I wish he would
come out to play.
Whatever does
he do all day?

Jane Clarke

Wobbly Tooth

Wiggerly wibberly
wobberly tooth,
it bibbles and bobbles,
I tell you the truth,
touch with your finger
and you will have proof
of my wiggerly wibberly
wobberly tooth!

John Prior

Wiggling

I've tried to wiggle every tooth,
But I've only got stiff teeth.
Are you sure that there are grown-up ones
Hidden underneath?

Michelle Magorian

Tickle

Tickle a ladybug,
tickle a flea,
tickle a pickle,
but don't tickle me.

Tickle an elephant,
tickle a worm,
but please, oh, please
don't make me squirm.

Don't tickle my elbows,
my ankles or knees,
my shoulders or ears—
ah ha ha *ha* PLEASE!

Eve Merriam

The Babysitter

When Mum and Dad go out to play
   with other dads and mums
before they've even said goodbye
   the Babysitter comes.

She doesn't seem to want to play
   with older girls and boys.
She'd rather come and bother me
   and play with all my toys.

I let her read my books and even
   ride me on her back.
I have to keep this girl amused
   till Mum and Dad get back.

I wouldn't mind this little job
   if I were paid a fee,
but when the Babysitter leaves
   it's *her* that's paid—not me!

Jez Alborough

83

Bath Time

Soap in the tub
slipple slapple slubble

Elbows and knees
scribble scrabble scrubble

Shampoo on head
bubble ubble bubble

Washcloth to squeeze
dribble drabble drubble

Water down the drain
spiggle spaggle spuggle

Water nearly gone
guggle uggle gluggle

Gurgle
    urgle
       gug

Eve Merriam

Shampoo Sally

Shampoo Sally
Washing her hair,
Splashing soapsuds everywhere.

Soapsuds in the water,
Soapsuds in the air,
Soapsuds here and soapsuds there.

Shampoo Sally
Rinsing her hair,
Splashing water everywhere.

Water on the bath mat,
Water on the floor,
Water dripping down the bathroom door.

Shampoo Sally
Washing her hair,
Soapsuds and water everywhere.
Shampoo Sally doesn't care.

John Foster

I Know It's Time

I know it's time
To say goodnight.
I know, it's time:
Turn out the light.

But I loved the one
With the princess proud,
And the one that made us
Laugh out loud.

I loved the one
About the bears,
And that other one
Where the Daddy cares—

And sometimes I
Could nearly cry,
'Cause I feel so full
And I don't know why

As here on the bed
We ride up high,
And the story goes on,
And the night goes by.

And one day I'll
Be big, I guess,
And I'll have some kids,
And I'll love them best

And I'll tell them the stories
You've told to me.
(But I'll love you still,
And I'll bring you tea . . .)

And now it's time:
Turn out the light.
I love you—it's time—
It's time . . . *Goodnight.*

Dennis Lee

Recipe For Sleep

One sleepy child
with nightlight glowing,
tucked up in bed
for a night-time poem.

A little drop of milk
warmed in a mug,
one favourite blanket
and one large hug.

A sprinkling of stars,
one rounded moon
dancing in a blackened sky
to light up the room.

One last ingredient
be sure not to miss—
blend it all together
with a goodnight kiss.

Tracey Blance

Acknowledgements

We are grateful to the authors for permission to include poems first published in this collection:

Tracey Blance: 'Recipe for Sleep', © Tracey Blance 2001. **Jane Clarke**: 'Hide and Seek' and 'Reflections', © Jane Clarke 2001. **John Coldwell**: 'The Cloud Dragon', © John Coldwell 2001. **Andrew Collett**: 'Bedtime at the Farmyard', © Andrew Collett 2001. **Sue Cowling**: 'Oh, Take me to the Seaside', © Sue Cowling 2001. **Richard Edwards** 'A Glance at the Menu', © Richard Edwards 2001. **Eric Finney**: 'What's in the Box?', © Eric Finney 2001. **John Foster**: 'Click Clack Jumping Jack', © John Foster 2001. **Pam Gidney**: 'Clap Your Hands', © Pam Gidney 2001. **Jean Kenward**: 'The Nest' and 'At Christmas', © Jean Kenward 2001. **Daphne Kitching**: 'Grandad's Greenhouse' and 'Adelaide Ida', © Daphne Kitching 2001. **John Kitching**: 'Plain to See?', © John Kitching 2001. **Patricia Leighton**: 'Fancy Dress Parade', © Patricia Leighton 2001. **J Patrick Lewis**: 'Sand Castle', © J Patrick Lewis 2001. **Tony Mitton**: 'Tiny Diny', © Tony Mitton 2001. **Brian Moses**: 'At the Playground', © Brian Moses 2001. **Frances Nagle**: 'Rock-a-bye', © Frances Nagle 2001. **Judith Nicholls**: 'Rainy Day Rumpus', © Judith Nicholls 2001. **Joan Poulson**: 'Jiggery Jaggery', © Joan Poulson 2001. **John Prior**: 'Wobbly Tooth', © John Prior 2001. **Cynthia Rider**: 'Jessica June', 'The Scary Fairies', and 'Fun in the Snow', © Cynthia Rider 2001. **Coral Rumble**: 'The Ballpool', © Coral Rumble 2001. **Roger Stevens**: 'Rain', © Roger Steens 2001. **Marian Swinger**: 'Noisy Food' and 'Mr Hullabaloo', © Marian Swinger 2001. **Jill Townsend**: 'Swinging', © Jill Townsend 2001. **Celia Warren**: 'Like Who...?', © Celia Warren 2001. **Brenda Williams**: 'Gloves ', © Brenda Williams 2001.

We are also grateful for permission to include the following published poems:

Georgie Adams: 'Green-Eyed Witches' and 'Mud' from Pumpkin Pie and Puddles (Orion). **John Agard**: 'Pumpkin, Pumpkin' from No Hickory, No Dickory, No Dock (Viking, 1991), reprinted by permission of the author c/o Caroline Sheldon Literary Agency. **Jez Alborough**: 'The Baby Sitter' from Shake Before Opening (Red Fox), reprinted by permission of The Random House Group Ltd. **Dorothy Aldis**: 'Dangerous' from All Together, copyright 1925-1928, 1934, 1939, 1952, renewed 1953, © 1954-1956, 1962 by Dorothy Aldis, © 1967 by Roy E Porter, renewed, reprinted by permission of G P Putnam's Sons, an imprint of Penguin Putnam Books for Young Readers, a division of Penguin Putnam Inc. **Giles Andreae**: 'Cow' from Cock-a-Doodle Do Farmyard Hullabaloo (1999), reprinted by permission of the publihsers, Orchard Books, a division of The Wattsd Publishing Group Limited, 96 Leonard Street, London EC2A 4XD. **Moira Andrew**: 'Christmas' from Rainbow Year (Belair Publications, 1994), 'How Far To Dreamland?' from Patchwork of Poems (Folens, 2000), and 'Winter Weather' first published in The Wider World edited by Robyn Gordon (Riverpoint Publishing, 1998), all poems © Moira Andrew, reprinted by permission of the author. **Clare Bevan**: 'Tarantula' first published in Poems about Animals (Wayland, 1999), reprinted by permission of the author. **Ann Bonner**: 'Riddle' first published in Playing with Words: Sound Effect Poems collected by Brian Moses (Pearson Education, 2000), reprinted by permission of the author.
Mark Burgess: 'Snow in the Lamplight' from Can't Get to Sleep (first published by Methuen Children's Books, an imprint of Egmont Children's Books Ltd, London), © 1990 Mark Burgess, reprinted by permission of the publishers. Charles Causley: 'High on the Wall' from Collected Poems 1951-2000 (Macmillan, 2000), reprinted by permission of David Higham Associates. **Lucy Coats**: 'I Met a Lion in the Park' and 'Fi! Fo! Fum! Fee!' from First Rhymes (Orchard Books, 1994), reprinted by permission of the author. **June Crebbin**: 'Holiday Memories' from The Dinosaur's Dinner (Viking, 1992), and 'Please-e!' from The Jungle Sale (Viking, 1988), both © June Crebbin, reprinted by permission of the author. **Edith E Cutting**: 'Snowman Snow' from Ladybug, January 1999, Vol 9, No 5, © 1999 by Edith E Cutting, reprinted by permission of Ladybug magazine, Cricket Magazine Group. **Richard Edwards**: 'If I were an Explorer' from If Only.. (Puffin, 1991), reprinted by permission of the author. **Max Fatchen**: 'Rockabye Baby' from Songs for My Dog and Other People (Puffin), reprinted by permission of John Johnson (Authors' Agent) Ltd. **John Foster**: 'One for the Pineapple' from Bouncing Ben and Other Rhymes (OUP, 1998), © John Foster 1998, and 'Shampoo Sally' from Doctor Proctor and Other Rhymes (OUP, 1998), © John Foster, reprinted by permission of the author. **Sue Graves**: 'There Once Was an Old Man from York' first published in Open House edited by John Cotton (Collins Educational, 1999), reprinted by permission of Harper Collins Publishers Ltd. **Margaret Hillert**: 'Blowing Bubbles' first published in The Walker Book of Read-Aloud Rhymes for the Very Young edited by Jack Prelutsky, reprinted by permission of the author. **Shirley Hughes**: 'Footprints' from Rhymes for Annie Rose (Red Fox), reprinted by permission of The Random House Group Ltd. **Jean Jaszi**: 'Lullaby' from Everybody Has Two Eyes (Lothrop Lee and Shepard). **Daphne Lister**: 'On Windy Days' from Gingerbread Pigs and Other Rhymes (Transworld, 1980), copyright © Daphne Lister 1980, reprinted by permission of the author. **Dennis Lee**: 'I Know It's Time' from The Ice Cream Store (HarperCollins Publishers Ltd, 1991), copyright © Dennis Lee 1991, reprinted by permission of the author c/o Westwod Creative Artists. **Michele Magorian**: 'What Would You Do?' and 'Wiggling' from Orange Paw Marks (Puffin). **Eve Merriam**: 'The Birthday Cow' from The Birthday Cow, copyright © 1978 Eve Merriam, 'Tickle' and 'Bath Time' from Higgle Wiggle (Mulberry Books, Morrow Jr), copyright © 1994 the Estate of Eve Merriam, reprinted by permission of Marian Reiner Literary Agent. **Tony Mitton**: 'Marvel Paws' from Marvel Paws (Cambridge University Press, 1996), reprinted by permission of the author. **Pamela Mordecai**: 'Grandma's House' from Story Poems: A First Collection (Ginn & Co, 1987), reprinted by permission of the author and the HSW Literary Agency. **Bob Morrow**: 'If I Were a Dog' from Spider, September 1998, Vol 5, No 9, © 1998 by Bob Morrow, reprinted by permission of Spider magazine, Cricket Magazine Group. **Grace Nichols**: 'Grasshopper One', copyright © Grace Nichols 1994, from Asana and the Animals: A Book of Pet Poems (Walker, 1997), reprinted by permission of Curtis Brown Ltd, London on behalf of Grace Nichols. **Hiawyn Oram**: 'Night Lights' and 'Only Human' from Speaking for Ourselves (Methuen Children's Books, 1990). **Jack Prelutsky**: 'Late One Night in Kalamazoo' from Ride a Purple Pelican (Greenwillow Books, 1986), © 1986 by Jack Prelutsky, reprinted by permission of HarperCollins Publishers (USA). **Irene Rawnsley**: 'Jiggery Street' first published in The Wider World edited by Robyn Gordon and Lynn Grey (Riverpoint Press, 1994), and 'Liquorice Bootlaces' from House of 100 Cats (Methuen Children's Books, 1995), both reprinted by permission of the author. **Cynthia Rider**: 'The Magic Carpet' from Magnificent Machines (Macmillan Children's Books, 2000), reprinted by permission of the author. Arthur Smith: 'Mister Frog' first published in The Big Book of Little Poems compiled by Roger McGough et al (Andre Deutsch, 1999), reprinted by permission of the author. **Kaye Umansky**: 'I Wish I was a Centipede' and 'Miss One ,Two and Three' from Nonsense Counting Rhymes (OUP, 1999), reprinted by permission of the author c/o Caroline Sheldon Literary Agency; 'Clumsy Clementina' first published in Food Rhymes edited by John Foster (OUP, 1998), reprinted by permission of the author. **Celia Warren**: 'Sounds Like Magic' first published in Senses Poems edited by John Foster (OUP, 1996), reprinted by permission of the author. **Brenda Williams**: 'Woodpecker' first published in Child Education magazine (Scholastic Ltd, June, 1999), reprinted by permisisonof the author.

Despite every effort to try to trace and contact copyright holders before publication this has not been possible in every case. If notified the publisher will be pleased to rectify any errors or omissions at the earliest opportunity.

Index of Artists

Cover illustration: **Tony Ross**

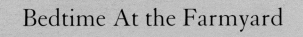

Bedtime At the Farmyard

It's bedtime at the farmyard
when the village clock strikes eight,
the chickens yawn and stretch
and the cows lock up the gate.

The geese all gather in the barn
to tell stories of the night,
the sheep close all the doors
and the pigs put out the light.

The turkeys tuck each other in
the ducks dream long and deep,
for when the village clock strikes eight
the farmyard falls asleep.

Andrew Collett